Jobs People

Pilots

by Mary Meinking

Raintree is an imprint of Capstone Global Library Limited, a company incorporated in England and Wales having its registered office at 264 Banbury Road, Oxford, OX2 7DY – Registered company number: 6695582

www.raintree.co.uk
myorders@raintree.co.uk

Text © Capstone Global Library Limited 2021
The moral rights of the proprietor have been asserted.

All rights reserved. No part of this publication may be reproduced in any form or by any means (including photocopying or storing it in any medium by electronic means and whether or not transiently or incidentally to some other use of this publication) without the written permission of the copyright owner, except in accordance with the provisions of the Copyright, Designs and Patents Act 1988 or under the terms of a licence issued by the Copyright Licensing Agency, Barnard's Inn, 86 Fetter Lane, London, EC4A 1EN (www.cla.co.uk). Applications for the copyright owner's written permission should be addressed to the publisher.

Edited by Gena Chester
Designed by Kyle Grenz
Original illustrations © Capstone Global Library Limited 2021
Picture research by Jo Miller
Production by Spencer Rosio
Originated by Capstone Global Library Ltd
Printed and bound in India

978 1 3982 0314 3 (hardback)
978 1 3982 0313 6 (paperback)

British Library Cataloguing in Publication Data
A full catalogue record for this book is available from the British Library.

Acknowledgements
We would like to thank the following for permission to reproduce photographs: Alamy: RichardBakerBA, 9; Newscom: Cultura/Zero Creatives, 25, TNS/Craig Kohlruss, 15; Shutterstock: Ceri Breeze, 12, ChameleonsEye, 16, depaz, 19, 4 PM production, 21 (left), Don Landwehrle, 13, Drew Horne, 18, EA Photography, 23, Jamen Percy, 6, Olena Yakobchuk, 7, RavenEyePhoto, 22, sirtravelot, 1, Skycolors, 10, 11, Sorbis, 5, Stokkete, Cover, supergenijalac, 17, zieusin, 27; U.S. Air Force photo by John Ingle, 26; U.S. Marine Corps photo by Sgt. Ashley Phillips, 14, 21 (right); Wikimedia: Library of Congress Prints and Photographs, 28

Every effort has been made to contact copyright holders of material reproduced in this book. Any omissions will be rectified in subsequent printings if notice is given to the publisher.

All the internet addresses (URLs) given in this book were valid at the time of going to press. However, due to the dynamic nature of the internet, some addresses may have changed, or sites may have changed or ceased to exist since publication. While the author and publisher regret any inconvenience this may cause readers, no responsibility for any such changes can be accepted by either the author or the publisher.

Contents

What is a pilot? 4

What pilots do 8

Where pilots work 12

How pilots help 16

Pilots' clothes and tools 20

How to become a pilot 24

Famous pilots 28

Fast facts 29

    Glossary 30

    Find out more 31

    Index 32

Words in **bold** are in the glossary.

What is a pilot?

An aeroplane speeds down the **runway**. You are pushed back in your seat. At the last second, the nose of the plane pops into the air. The plane lifts off the ground. You're flying!

Pilots are the people who fly planes. They sit at the front in the **cockpit**. They fly along a planned path. Then they land the plane safely.

5

Pilots need to work well with others. They can fly one person or they can fly hundreds of people.

Have you flown in a plane? Did you like it? All pilots love to fly.

7

What pilots do

Airline pilots have to be at the airport an hour before their flights. They write the flight plan. They look at the weather. They decide which way to go.

Pilots check inside and outside the plane. They make sure planes fly safely.

Then they check everything in the cockpit. They check the fuel, propeller and lights. Everything is ready! The plane leaves the gate. They drive the plane to the runway and wait to take off.

9

It's time for take-off! The pilot pulls back on the controls. The plane speeds down the runway. The plane lifts off. It is in the air! When the plane is going in the right direction, the pilot turns on **autopilot**.

Pilots turn off autopilot when the plane nears the airport. They bring the plane in lower. It goes over the runway. The wheels touch down. Pilots put on the breaks. The plane rolls to the gate.

Airline pilots fly about 75 hours every month. They spend 150 hours a month getting ready for their flights.

Where pilots work

Pilots work all around the world. They fly many types of planes.

Some pilots fly boat planes. They can only take off and land on water.

A woman getting off a boat plane

A crop duster plane

Some pilots fly crop duster planes. They fly low over farmers' fields. They spray crops with **chemicals** to kill pests and weeds.

A pilot in the US Marine Corps

Pilots can fly for the **military**. Some fly in battles. Others carry supplies or troops. Some carry doctors, nurses or injured soldiers. A few look for the enemy from their planes.

Other pilots fly **cargo** planes. They carry letters, boxes and other items. They go all over the world.

This cargo plane is carrying shelter dogs.

How pilots help

Pilots help people around the world. They take people from place to place. Pilots can also carry things people need. They can drop water, food and supplies. **Parachutes** float these things to the ground.

A plane drops supplies.

A tanker plane sprays chemicals over a fire.

Some pilots fight fires. They fly tanker planes that drop water on forest fires. They can also spray chemicals. This helps to stop the fire. Other planes carry firefighters. Firefighters parachute out of planes near fires. They fight fires from the ground.

Helicopter pilots help people too. Helicopters fly where planes can't go.

Some helicopter pilots fly sick or injured people. They take them to hospital.

A helicopter lands at a hospital.

A rescue crew flying a helicopter

Helicopter pilots help find lost people. They fly low to spot them. At night, they shine bright lights on the ground.

Some helicopter pilots help rescue people. They pull people out of the water, forests or mountains.

Pilots' clothes and tools

Airline pilot's **uniforms** look like military uniforms. Most pilots wear dark blue or black jackets and trousers. They wear a white shirt and tie. Some pilots also wear a hat.

Airline pilots wear a pin with wings. Stripes are on their shoulders and wrists. Head pilots or captains wear four stripes. Co-pilots wear three stripes.

Pilots who fly for the military wear flight suits. Flight suits are worn over their clothes. They protect pilots from fires.

An airline pilot

A military pilot

21

Pilots control the whole plane from the cockpit. The dashboard and ceiling has many switches, buttons and computers. Each one controls a different part of the plane.

dashboard

radar screen

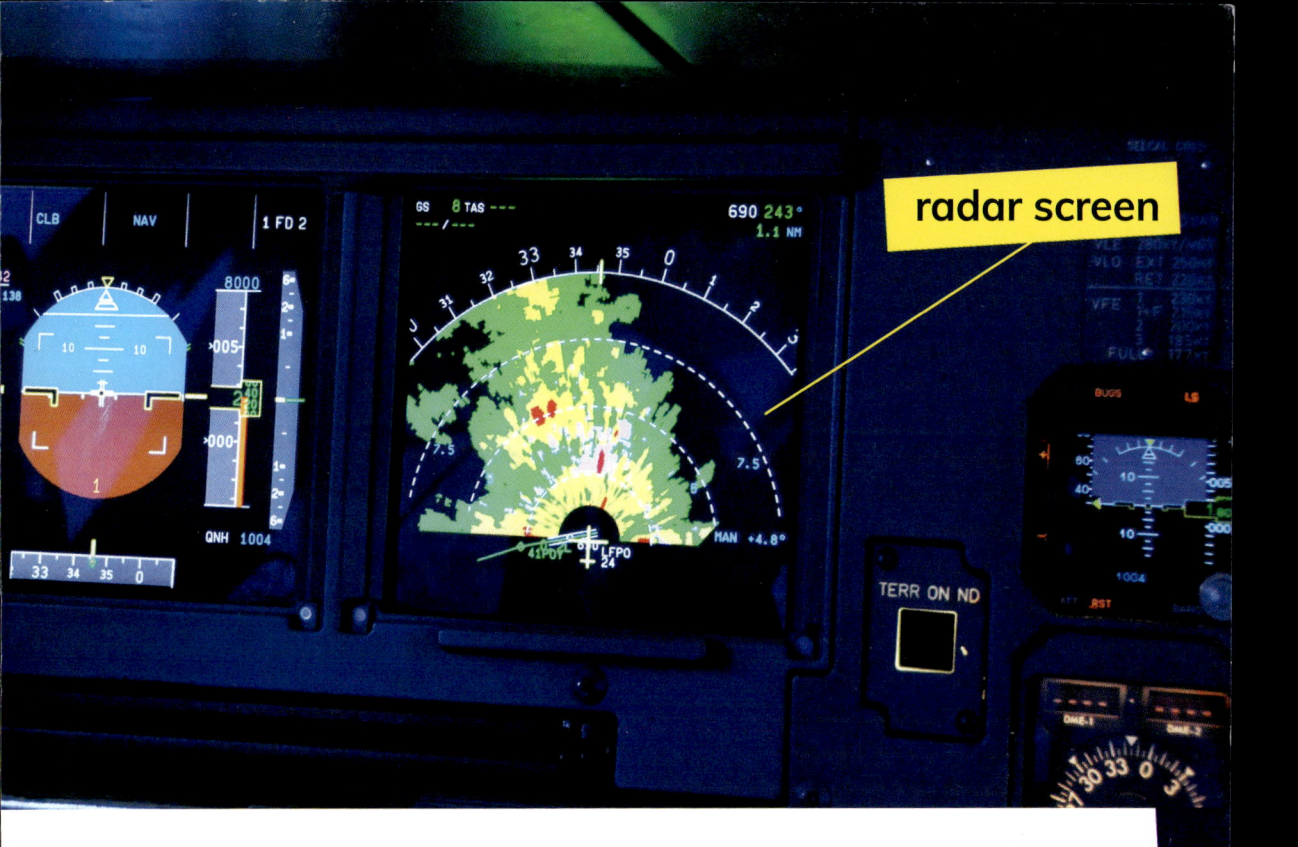

Airline pilots have **rudder** pedals. A rudder moves the plane right and left. Pilots use a control column. This makes the plane go up and down.

During the flight, autopilot flies the plane. Pilots watch the **radar** screen. It shows the weather and other aircraft in the sky.

How to become a pilot

Pilots can work privately. They can also work for airlines. Many pilots are co-pilots or teachers.

There are many steps to becoming a pilot. Pilots must be at least 18 years old.

Future pilots can go to flying school. There they take written tests. They practise flying in a flight **simulator** before they fly in real planes. With enough real flight hours, pilots can become captains.

To fly bigger planes, pilots need more training. They need to track more flight hours. There are more tests to pass.

Future pilots can also join the military. They need a degree to become an officer. They need to pass tests. Then they get pilot training. They track thousands of hours flying.

A future Air Force pilot practising in a flight simulator

If pilots leave the military, they can work for an airline. Airlines employ many military pilots.

Famous pilots

In 1903, the Wright brothers flew the first powered plane. The wooden framed wings were covered in fabric. It was in the air for 12 seconds.

Tuskegee Airmen were the first African American military pilots. They fought in World War II. Their success helped other African Americans become pilots.

Tuskegee Airmen

Fast facts

- **What pilots do:**
They fly aircraft.

- **Where pilots work:**
airlines, military, private companies

- **Key clothing:**
blue or black uniform, a winged pin, flight suit

- **Key tools:**
aircraft, radar screen, rudder, control column

- **Education needed:**
flight school or military, written tests

- **Famous pilots:**
the Wright Brothers, Tuskegee Airmen

Glossary

autopilot device that controls aircraft

cargo objects carried by an aircraft

chemical substance used to put out fires

cockpit place where a pilot sits in a plane

military armed forces of a state or country

parachute something that allows people to safely jump from high places

radar device that uses radio waves to track the location of objects

rudder flat piece of metal attached to a plane that is used for steering

runway long, flat strip of ground where an aircraft can take off or land

simulator device that recreates what something looks like and how it happens in real life; simulators are used for training, before moving on to the real thing

uniform special clothes that members of a particular group wear

Find out more

Books

Audacious Aviators: True Stories of Adventurers' Thrilling Flights (Ultimate Adventurers), Jen Green (Raintree, 2015)

The Big Book of Planes: Discover the Biggest, Fastest and Best Flying Machines, DK (DK Children, 2020)

The Careers Handbook: The ultimate guide to planning your future, DK (DK Children, 2019)

Websites

www.bbc.co.uk/bitesize/topics/zvb76v4/articles/zdcskmn
Learn more about famous aviators.

www.dkfindout.com/uk/transport/history-aircraft
Find out more about the history of aircraft.

Index

autopilot 10, 11, 23

boat planes 12

captains 20, 24
cargo planes 15
chemicals 13, 17
cockpits 4, 8, 22
co-pilots 20, 24
crop duster planes 13

education 24

flight hours 11, 24, 25, 26
flight suits 20
fuel 8

helicopters 18, 19

lights 8, 19

militaries 14, 20, 26, 27, 28

parachutes 16, 17
paths 4
pedals 23
plans 8
propellers 8

radars 23
runways 4, 8, 10, 11

simulators 24

tanker planes 17
tests 24, 25, 26
Tuskegee Airmen 28

uniforms 20

Wright brothers, the 28